ENERGY SOURCES

Solar Power

by Tracy Vonder Brink

A Crabtree Crown Book

CRABTREE
Publishing Company
www.crabtreebooks.com

School-to-Home Support for Caregivers and Teachers

This appealing book is designed to teach students about core subject areas. Students will build upon what they already know about the subject, and engage in topics that they want to learn more about. Here are a few guiding questions to help readers build their comprehension skills. Possible answers appear here in red.

Before Reading:

What do I know about solar power?
- *I know the Sun makes light.*
- *I know the Sun makes heat.*

What do I want to learn about this topic?
- *I want to know how solar power makes electricity.*
- *I want to learn how solar panels work.*

During Reading:

I'm curious to know...
- *I'm curious to know how solar power heats a home.*
- *I'm curious to know how many solar power systems the United States has.*

How is this like something I already know?
- *I know how my home is heated.*
- *I have seen solar panels.*

After Reading:

What was the author trying to teach me?
- *The author was trying to teach me what solar power is.*
- *The author was trying to teach me how solar power can replace fossil fuels.*

How did the photographs and captions help me understand more?
- *The photographs helped me understand how solar power systems work.*
- *The captions gave me extra information.*

Table of Contents

Chapter 1: Energy and Fuel

We need energy for everything we do. Energy heats our homes. Our bodies use it to live. It fuels our cars. But what is energy?

In science, work is energy moving from one object to another. Your feet pushing against your bike's pedals are doing work that makes the bike move.

Energy is the ability to do work or to make something happen. Energy is everywhere. It comes in different forms. Heat, light, and sound are all forms of energy. The lights in your home use electrical energy.

Transforming Energy

Energy can be transformed, or changed, from one form to another. Energy changes forms when it is used to make something happen. Wood has energy locked inside it. Burning the wood changes its energy into heat and light.

Heat and light are two forms of energy.

A fuel is something that is changed in some way to produce energy. Wood is a fuel because burning it releases heat and light. Food is fuel for your body. Your body breaks down what you eat and uses it as energy.

Fossil Fuels

Fossil fuels are nonrenewable energy sources. Nonrenewable means they cannot be replaced.

We use fuels to make heat and power. Coal, oil, and natural gas are fuels. They are burned to release their energy. They all come from underneath the ground and they formed over millions of years. These types of fuels are called fossil fuels. If we use them up, they cannot be replaced.

Climate Change

Fossil fuels give off **carbon dioxide** when they are burned. Carbon dioxide collects in a layer around Earth. This layer traps heat and warms the planet. As Earth becomes warmer, its **climate** changes. We need energy sources that will not run out and that will not change the climate. We need **alternative** sources of energy. One such source is solar power.

Climate change harms people and animals. Impacts of climate change include higher temperatures and changes in rainfall. This can lead to wildfires and less water for crops. These changes affect where people and animals live and the food that they eat.

The Sun is a hot ball of gas more than 300,000 times bigger than Earth. The core is the Sun's center. Its energy comes from its core. The Sun's core is about 27 million °Fahrenheit (15 million °C).

Elements in the Sun's core fuse together over and over and release massive amounts of energy. That energy travels through space. It reaches Earth as light and heat. We cannot take energy out of sunlight, but we can use it in a different way.

Chapter 3: Reflecting Sunlight

Archimedes, a Greek inventor, is said to have defeated attacking Roman ships with sunlight in 212 B.C.E. He reflected sunlight from polished shields and set their ships on fire.

Ancient Greeks and Romans sometimes **reflected** sunlight from polished metal mirrors to light torches. In 1782, French scientist Antoine Lavoisier used sunlight and glass to produce a temperature of 3000 °Fahrenheit (1649 °C). Today's solar thermal **power plants** use the same idea.

This solar thermal power plant is near Seville, Spain.

Solar Thermal Power Plants

Any smooth surface that bounces light back can be used as a mirror. That is why you can see yourself in a pond's still water.

A mirror is glass coated with silver or aluminum on one side. When light hits the mirror's surface, it reflects. Solar thermal power plants use mirrors to reflect sunlight.

Power Tower Plant

A power tower plant is one kind of solar thermal power plant. Mirrors are placed in a circle around the tower. Computers track the Sun and shift the mirrors so the reflected sunlight always hits the top of the tower.

A power tower plant in California's Mojave Desert uses more than 100,000 mirrors.

The top of the tower is filled with **fluid**. The fluid heats when the light from the mirrors hits it. The hot fluid travels from the tower to another part of the power plant.

Mirrors focus sunlight onto a receiver at the top of a tower at a solar plant.

Making Electricity

Other solar thermal power plants use mirrors in a dish or in a long row. All use focused sunlight to heat fluid and turn a generator.

The hot fluid is used to boil water like a giant teakettle. Boiling water releases steam. The steam pushes against blades connected to a **generator**. The blades turn, and the generator makes electricity. One solar thermal power plant may create enough electricity to power about 90,000 homes.

A generator is a machine that turns motion into electricity.

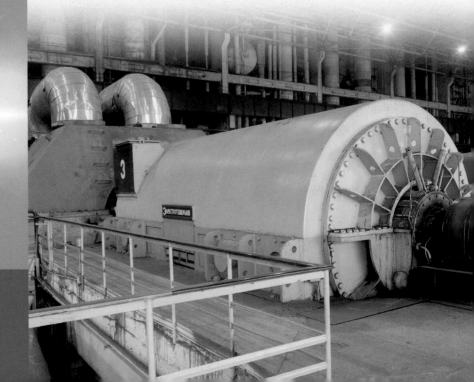

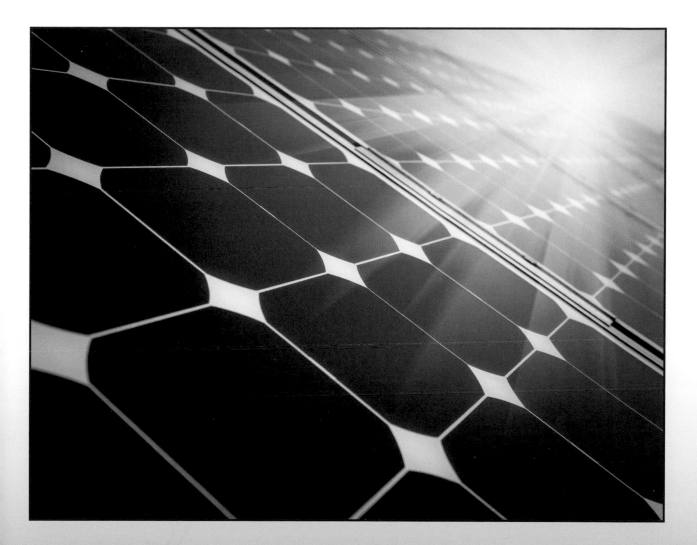

Solar panels do not have mirrors, so how do they make electricity? Instead of reflecting sunlight, solar panels use it to create electrical energy. Smaller sets of solar panels make enough electricity for a house or a business. Large solar farms may power millions.

Solar panels on solar farms are made up of solar cells. These cells contain layers that are used to create electricity. Sunlight contains energy. When that energy hits a solar cell, its layers generate electrical energy.

A large solar farm may have more than 1 million solar panels.

Rooftop Solar Panels

Solar panels on buildings work the same way as those on solar farms. These solar panels send electricity directly into the home. Some home solar systems have batteries to store electricity for later use.

Chapter 5: Powering a City

Electricity in a power grid may come from both nonrenewable and alternative energy sources.

Electricity from a solar farm travels through power lines to a **substation**. The substation changes the electricity into a form that can be sent to a **power grid**. All sources of electricity feed into the same power grids.

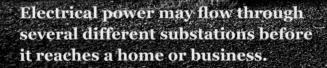

Electrical power may flow through several different substations before it reaches a home or business.

Smaller substations carry the electricity to towns and cities. Power lines above or below the ground connect them. Electricity flows from the substation into homes, businesses, streetlights, and more.

Solar parks are solar power plants grouped in the same area. China's Golmud Solar Park has 80 solar power plants.

Today, the United States has more than 3 million solar power systems. Many are solar panels on houses. These solar power systems produce enough electricity for more than 18 million homes.

In the United States, the southwestern states receive the most sunlight. California has the most solar power systems of any state.

Sunlight Needed

Solar power systems must have sunlight to work. They produce less electricity on stormy days, and none is made overnight. Not all places are sunny enough to collect solar energy. Winter sunlight is also weaker than in the summer months. Tall buildings, trees, and even mountain ranges may block sunlight.

Cost to Build

The cost of solar panels has dropped, but they are still expensive. A solar farm may cost between 800,000 dollars and 2 million dollars to build. China spent as much as 2 billion dollars on one of its large solar parks.

Solar panels must be installed by professionals.

A home solar panel system costs between 15,000 dollars and 25,000 dollars. A homeowner who also wants a battery to store extra electricity may spend another 7,000 dollars to 14,000 dollars.

Land Needed

The amount of sunlight reaching any one spot on Earth is fairly small, so solar power farms must be built over large areas of land. The land also needs to be flat. One of the concerns about large solar farms is that they take land away from people and animals.

Other Problems

Solar panels rarely break, but when they do, replacing a broken solar panel can cost thousands of dollars.

Solar energy releases no carbon dioxide, but factories that make solar panels do. Solar thermal power plants need a lot of water to work. Some people worry that solar farms harm wildlife, such as birds.

Chapter 7: The Future of Solar Power

Solar power is clean energy, and sunlight is free. The amount of sunlight that hits Earth in less than two hours is enough to power the world for one year. Solar panels on an area about the size of Lake Michigan could supply enough electricity for all of the United States.

Solar power is the third most widely used alternative energy source in the world today. However, it still makes less than 10 percent of the world's electricity and 4 percent of the electricity in the United States. Will solar power be the future's alternative energy source?

Glossary

alternative (ahl-TUR-nuh-tive): Something that may be chosen instead of something else

carbon dioxide (CAR-bun dye-OX-ide): A gas that is produced when people or animals breathe out or when certain fuels are burned

climate (KLEYE-muht): The usual weather conditions of a particular place

element (EH-luh-muhnt): A pure substance made from a single type of atom

fluid (FLOO-uhd): A liquid

generator (JEH-nuh-ray-tr): A machine that changes movement into electricity

power grid (PAU-ur GRID): A connected system for delivering electrical power from power plants to homes and businesses

power plant (PAU-ur PLANT): A place where electricity is made

reflect (ruh-FLEKT): Light bouncing off an object, as in a mirror

substation (SUHB-stay-shn): Equipment that makes electricity usable for people

Index

Comprehension Questions

1. How does a tower power plant use sunlight?
   a. Mirrors on the top of a tower collect sunlight
   b. Mirrors reflect sunlight to the top of the tower
   c. The top of the tower changes sunlight to electricity

2. What happens when sunlight hits a solar panel?
   a. Layers in the solar cells generate electricity
   b. Layers in the solar cells reflect sunlight
   c. Layers in the solar cells heat fluid

3. What is one of the challenges of solar power?
   a. Solar power uses a lot of land
   b. Solar panels break easily
   c. Solar power will run out

4. True or False: Nonrenewable energy sources can be replaced.

5. True or False: Solar energy is clean energy.

Comprehension questions answer key: 1. b 2. a 3. a 4. False 5. True

About the Author

Tracy Vonder Brink loves true stories and facts. She has written more than 20 books for kids and is a contributing editor for three children's science magazines. Tracy lives in Cincinnati, Ohio, with her husband, two daughters, and two rescue dogs.

Written by: Tracy Vonder Brink
Designed by: Jennifer Bowers
Series Development: James Earley
Proofreader: Melissa Boyce
Educational Consultant: Marie Lemke M.Ed.
Print Coordinator: Katherine Berti

Photographs: cover and p.19 ©2020 Wirestock Creators/Shutterstock, ©R2D2/Shutterstock; p.4 ©2021 Lin Xiu Xiu/Shutterstock; p.5 ©2015 Africa Studio/Shutterstock; p.6 ©2020 Natalia Leinonen/Shutterstock; p.7 ©2016 Tatjana Baibakova/Shutterstock; p8. ©2020 Sunshine Seeds/Shutterstock; p.9 ©2009 Mark Smith/Shutterstock; p.10 ©2019 Lukasz Pawel Szczepanski/Shutterstock; p.11 ©2013 KingJC/Shutterstock; p.12 ©2019 Fly_and_Dive/Shutterstock; p.13 ©2012 Cristina Romero Palma/Shutterstock; p.14 ©2019 Fly_and_Dive/Shutterstock; p.15 ©2012 Raul Baena/Shutterstock; p.16 ©2010 rtem/Shutterstock; p.17 ©2015 chinasong/Shutterstock; p.18 ©2017 Fly_and_Dive/Shutterstock; p.20-21 ©2017 Jenson/Shutterstock; p.22 ©2021 DBHAVSAR/Shutterstock; p.23 ©2013 Svitlana Kazachek/Shutterstock; p.24 ©2020 BELL KA PANG/Shutterstock; p.25 ©2010 Elena Elisseeva/Shutterstock; p.26 ©2017 zhangyang13576997233/Shutterstock; p.27 ©2019 Altrendo Images/Shutterstock; p.28-29 ©2020 Fit Ztudio/Shutterstock

Library and Archives Canada Cataloguing in Publication

Available at the Library and Archives Canada

Library of Congress Cataloging-in-Publication Data

Available at the Library of Congress

Crabtree Publishing Company

www.crabtreebooks.com   1-800-387-7650

Copyright © 2023 **CRABTREE PUBLISHING COMPANY**

Published in the United States
Crabtree Publishing
347 Fifth Avenue
Suite 1402-145
New York, NY, 10016

Published in Canada
Crabtree Publishing
616 Welland Ave.
St. Catharines, ON
L2M 5V6

Printed in the U.S.A./072022/CG20220201